HOW I
BUILT A BANK
AND STILL
REMAINED
POOR

HOW I
BUILT A BANK
AND STILL
REMAINED
POOR

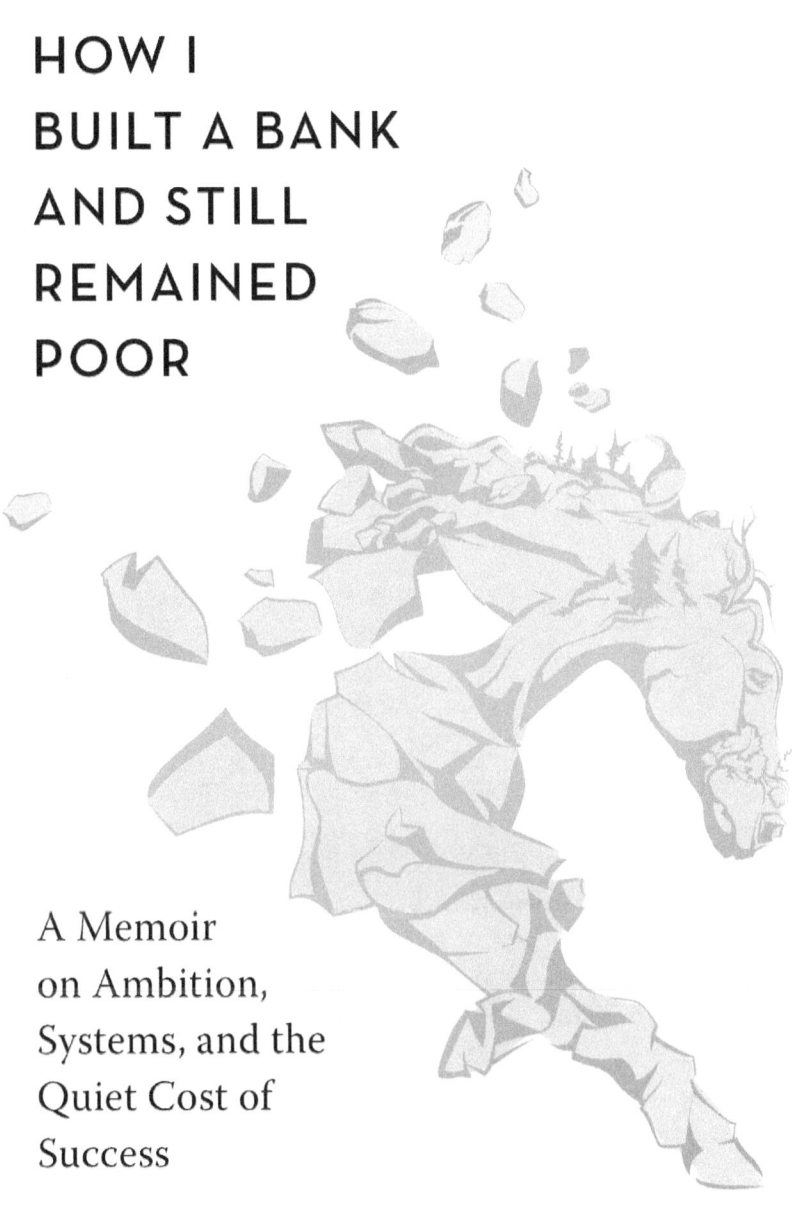

A Memoir
on Ambition,
Systems, and the
Quiet Cost of
Success

JAMES ROBERTS

Published by ARINA LLC
Sacramento, California, USA
ISBN: 979-8-9940206-1-6
Printed and distributed via IngramSpark.

DEDICATION

This book is the product of many journeys — across countries, institutions, and seasons of my life. I am deeply grateful to the people who walked with me, challenged me, encouraged me, and ultimately helped me find clarity long before I found the words to tell this story.

To the extraordinary colleagues and friends I met across **Zimbabwe, Kenya, Zambia, Ghana, Nigeria, Cameroon, London, The Gambia, and beyond** — thank you for shaping my professional and personal growth in ways I could never have foreseen. Your brilliance, resilience, and humanity left an imprint on me that continues to inspire my work today.

To the leaders who believed in my abilities long before I fully understood them myself — thank you for the opportunities, the trust, and the lessons. Some were loud, many were quiet, but each one helped me step into the fullness of my potential.

To the people who shared the long nights, the system failures, the high-stakes deadlines, the tense boardrooms, and the triumphant breakthroughs — you taught me the value of teamwork, character, and integrity. You made the journey bearable, meaningful, and unforgettable.

To my family — whose patience, love, and steady presence kept me centered through every transition — I owe more than these pages can hold.

And to you, the reader — thank you for opening this book and stepping into my story. May it remind you that your life is worth more than titles, salaries, or metrics, and that peace is the greatest wealth you will ever own.

FOREWORD

When James first shared parts of this manuscript with me, I immediately recognized something rare: a story that speaks not only to the technical and operational realities of multinational banking, but to the inner life of the people who keep those systems functioning.

For over two decades, I have worked within financial services, specializing in card payments, digital platforms, and operational resilience. I have observed talented individuals rise through the ranks, only to discover later that success in corporate life can be both empowering and disorienting. Very few, however, have articulated this journey with the clarity and honesty found in these pages.

James writes with the precision of an engineer and the empathy of someone who has led teams, mentored younger professionals, and carried the silent weight of decisions that shape institutions. His reflections are not theoretical. They are lived. They come from late nights in server rooms, from tense boardrooms, from crisis calls across borders, and from the deeply human moments that rarely make it into official reports.

What makes this book important is not merely what James accomplished — though his career spans multiple countries, complex projects, and a rare breadth of responsibility. What makes it important is what he learned and how those lessons can guide the next generation.

Young professionals entering global institutions will find in this memoir both a warning and a guide:

- **A warning** that competence alone does not guarantee fulfillment.

- **A guide** showing how to build a life — not just a résumé — with integrity, intention, and balance.

For leaders, this book is a mirror. For institutions, it is a reminder that human capital is more fragile than balance sheets suggest. And for anyone seeking meaning beyond metrics, this is a story of rediscovery.

It is my privilege to introduce this work.

James has built systems, teams, and bank branches — but in these pages, he builds something even more valuable: perspective.

— *Ernest Kapaya BSc, MSc*
Cards Payment Specialist

PREFACE

This book did not begin as a memoir. It began as a collection of quiet reflections written long after I left the world that shaped me. For years, I believed my career was defined by projects completed, systems built, crises resolved, and promotions earned. Only later did I understand that the true story — the one worth telling — lived beneath the surface of those events.

Corporate life, especially in multinational banking, has a way of convincing you that your identity is inseparable from your output. I believed this too. I wore my responsibilities like armor and treated my achievements as currency. But as the years unfolded, I discovered that the real lessons were not in the systems I stabilized or the institutions I served. They were in the quiet moments: the cost of loyalty, the erosion of self, the rediscovery of purpose, and the realization that peace is a greater wealth than salary or stature.

This book is not a critique of banking. It is, instead, a human story set against the backdrop of banking — a story of ambition, misalignment, courage, awakening, and ultimately, freedom. It is a message to young professionals who are entering systems that will demand more of them than they expect, and to seasoned leaders who may have forgotten the cost of the journey.

Every chapter reflects a truth I learned not from textbooks, but from people — colleagues, customers, managers, and mentors — in regions as diverse as Accra, Nairobi, Lagos, Harare, London, and beyond. Some names and locations have been generalized intentionally, not to obscure the truth, but to universalize the experience.

If this book does anything, I hope it reminds you of one thing:

Your career is not your life.

Your title is not your identity.

And your peace is not negotiable.

— *James Roberts*

CONTENTS

CHAPTER 1

THE UNPLANNED BEGINNING

Most careers begin with intention. Mine began with interruption.

When I walked out of The University of Buckingham, UK with a degree in Computer Science with Economics, I imagined a smooth entry into research, data, or healthcare systems. I had spent the previous years post-high school, in Life Sciences and medical pathology particularly. What drove me to computers was to prepare for a new digital era beginning in the late 1980s. Why Economics? I was clueless about money and business at the time. Therefore, I was preparing for a path that made intellectual sense. Yet, as life often does, opportunity arrived from an unexpected direction.

I joined the banking sector almost reluctantly—an analyst role that felt, at the time, like a temporary compromise rather than a step toward a career. The job promised stability, a predictable income, and a respectable name on my résumé. I told myself it was a bridge, not a destination. What I didn't realize was that this "temporary" decision would become a defining doorway—one that would shape the next twenty years of my life.

The banking world was loud, structured, and intimidating. I traded lab reports for call logs, system diagrams for service queues, and quiet academic routines for the relentless hum of corporate urgency. Everything felt unfamiliar: the metrics, the expectations, the language. I had to start again—not just at a junior level, but at a junior level in a field I had never imagined entering.

Yet in the chaos, something inside me awoke.

I discovered that solving problems for people—real customers, real teams—brought a satisfaction I had not found in theory. The systems were messy, often frustrating, sometimes outdated, but always fascinating. Every day was a puzzle. And I learned quickly: the bank rewarded speed, precision, and people who could stay calm when things broke.

My early days were humble. Small tasks. Small wins. Endless learning. But there was something quietly forming in the background: a discipline, an instinct, a recognition of how systems behave—not in textbooks, but in the real world, under pressure.

This chapter of my life began without ambition. Yet it planted seeds that would grow into something far larger, more complex, and ultimately more personal than I could ever have predicted.

I was not just entering a bank.

I was entering a system that would change me.

THE MAKING OF A PROFESSIONAL

If Chapter 1 marked the beginning of my entry into banking, Chapter 2 marked the moment I began to understand the systems and the people. The bank was more than computers, ATMs, and service desks. It was a living organism—imperfect, fragile, dependent on the constant movement of people who barely realized the role they played. As an analyst, I sat at the intersection of everything: customers demanding solutions, branches escalating issues, and managers requiring reports. It was chaotic. But beneath the noise, patterns emerged.

**Where systems failed, people filled the gaps.
And where people failed, systems collapsed.**

This was my first real lesson: technology alone doesn't keep a bank running—people do. Good systems fail in the hands of poorly trained staff, and even bad systems can thrive under the attention of competent teams.

I became obsessed with identifying weaknesses. Not to expose anyone, but because I genuinely wanted to fix things. I watched how calls came in, how staff responded, how customers reacted, and how problems escalated. Every interaction told a story about the deeper health of the institution.

Soon, I was documenting common faults, mapping recurring failures, and proposing fixes. My notes were not fancy. They were written on scraps of paper, the backs of printouts, margins of call logs. But managers noticed something: I could connect dots others missed. I remember in those early days, setting a weekly system support target of "Zero Down-Time" where hitherto, system outages would occur multiple times during the week and sometimes, during the same business day, much to the frustration of customers and staff.

THE DAY EVERYTHING SHIFTED

A regional manager once asked me why a particular service issue kept recurring in three branches across the municipality. I explained—not with corporate jargon, but with clarity. I highlighted patterns, system gaps, training deficiencies, and operational inconsistencies.

He stared at me for a moment and said quietly, "You see the system behind the system."

That sentence changed the trajectory of my career.

Suddenly, I was no longer the junior analyst helping frontline teams. I was the young man who could explain why things went wrong before they became headlines. The bank was beginning to see my value—before I fully understood it myself.

TEACHING THE SYSTEM

My ability to break down complexity into simple concepts made me a natural trainer. I started leading small sessions to help staff understand the logic behind the systems they used daily. It wasn't long before those sessions grew into structured training programs.

I taught people how to prevent fraud by understanding system behaviors.

I taught branches how to avoid errors by anticipating the consequences of each transactionor account setting.

I taught young analysts how to read logs, trace faults, and "listen" to systems the way doctors listen to patients.

Training revealed another truth:
knowledge, when shared, multiplies.

And the more I shared, the more the bank trusted me.

SMALL VICTORIES THAT BUILT A FOUNDATION

I was still young, still learning, still stumbling. But each small victory—a resolved crisis, a faster system, a cleaner process—built a foundation I didn't yet recognize as the start of something bigger.

Looking back, this period was where I grew up professionally.

It wasn't glamorous.

It wasn't strategic.

It was simply work—hard, demanding work.

But it shaped me.

It sharpened me.

It prepared me for roles I could never have imagined then.

These early lessons—about systems, people, patterns, and leadership—would later carry me through multi-country responsibilities, high-stress deployments, and rooms filled with senior executives. But at the time, I was simply trying to be useful.

What I didn't know was that the bank had begun watching.

And soon, they would move me far beyond my comfort zone.

CHAPTER 3

THE RISE THROUGH THE SYSTEM

Rising through the banking world didn't happen in a moment. It happened in layers—quietly, gradually, almost unnoticed. One challenging task, then another. One successful project, then another. Yet each step forward came with a shadow attached to it, a subtle reminder that progress in multinational institutions is never as simple as competence alone.

My move into regional service management marked a turning point. I was still young, still finding my way, but I had already become known for one thing: I could see the system behind the system. I could trace problems to their origins, anticipate failures before they erupted, and explain complexity in a way that demystified it for others. That reputation earned me greater responsibility—and with it came the constant travel.

A LIFE LIVED IN AIRPORTS

Nairobi one week.

Mombasa the next.

Cameroon after that.

Ghana, Nigeria, London occasionally and The Gambia.

Airports became my second home. I learned the choreography of transit: security lines, boarding zones, taxi queues, late-night hotel check-ins, and early-morning presentations. I measured my life not in months, but in layovers.

To outsiders, it looked glamorous.

To me, it often felt like survival.

Travel revealed the true nature of multinational operations: under-resourced teams trying to meet global expectations; legacy systems patched together to satisfy modern demands; entire branches relying on committed staff doing their best. I met extraordinary people—men and women who held banks together with dedication the public would never see.

THE ILLUSION OF CONTROL

My title grew. So did my inbox.

I ran regional dashboards, service reviews, and crisis calls. And in every country I visited, staff looked at me as "the guy from head office" — the one who brought answers, pressure, or both.

But promotions bring more visibility, and visibility brings politics.

I learned quickly that success in multinational banking is not simply about what you know or even what you do. It is also about:

- who hears your ideas,
- who champions your work,
- and who remembers your name in meetings you are not invited to.

Competence mattered—but it wasn't the whole story.

THE POWER OF THE SLIDE DECK

I spent countless hours building presentations: slides full of metrics, dashboards, red-amber-green indicators, recommendations, timelines, risks, and post-implementation reviews. I once produced a 30-slide deck summarizing a major system upgrade. The team behind it had spent nights in server rooms, but their names never appeared. Only mine did.

During the quarterly review, a senior executive presented the deck—my deck—to the global board without mentioning my contribution. He accepted the applause with a smile.

I said nothing.

But something inside me shifted.

It was my first real lesson in the politics of visibility: **credit flows upward, not downward.**

LEARNING TO NAVIGATE POWER

A mentor once told me, "In this system, you must learn to be visible without being loud, and indispensable without being dangerous." It took me years to understand what he meant.

Being visible meant speaking up at the right time.

Being indispensable meant solving problems nobody else could.

Being safe meant never outshining those above you too brightly.

I walked that tightrope for years.

BURNOUT DISGUISED AS ACHIEVEMENT

Travel, pressure, and constant delivery came at a cost I did not immediately see. I was celebrated for my work ethic, but privately, I was exhausted. I missed birthdays. I missed family milestones. I lived out of bags. And yet, I convinced myself that this was the price of progress—"paying dues" for a better future.

Burnout doesn't shout.

It whispers, slowly, through fatigue you learn to normalize.

But even then, I felt a growing emptiness:

Was I building a future for myself?

Or was I building stability for institutions that would replace me within a week if I vanished?

A MOMENT OF CLARITY

During a late-night stopover in Dubai, staring at my reflection in a glass wall of the departures hall, I realized I was running—running to deliver, to prove myself, to remain relevant. But in that race, I had lost track of something far more important: ownership.

I was contributing value to shareholders I had never met.

I was strengthening institutions I did not own.

I was shaping systems that gave me a salary, but not security.

That realization did not arrive with anger. It arrived with clarity.

THE MAN I WAS BECOMING

I had gained confidence, expertise, and recognition.

But I had also gained distance—from myself, from my own planning, from the life I imagined as a young graduate.

Chapter 3 closed with a truth I could no longer ignore:

I had risen through the system, but I had not risen within myself.

The climb was real.

But so was the cost.

CHAPTER 4

THE ARCHITECT OF SECURITY

By my thirteenth year in banking, I had earned a reputation I never applied for:

the one who could make chaos orderly.

A Senior Project Manager once asked me, *"James How come you're always so cool when there are problems all over the place?" He asked the question with his trademark smile. I did not reply. I* simply smiled and moved on with my clip board in hand.

To lead in technology, you must first bring order.

And so, whenever a system failed or an audit trail revealed anomalies, my phone rang. I had become the unofficial architect of security — not the kind that builds vaults or alarm systems, but the kind that builds trust in invisible structures.

My responsibility expanded quickly. I had to assemble a team of true specialists — telecoms experts, security analysts, server engineers — people who could see the same invisible faults I did. Together, we protected the bank's computing assets from unauthorized access. The work was constant, precise, and mostly unnoticed — the kind of success that leaves no trace.

THE ASSIGNMENT THAT DEFINED ME

It began with a crisis.

The bank's subsidiary in Sierra Leone had been closed for a year during the long civil war (1991–2002). The institution was on the brink of permanent shutdown. And once again, I was the *Fixer*.

In November 1998, during a rare lull in the fighting, I landed in Freetown on the only airline still willing to resume flights to Lungi Airport. From there, I boarded an old Russian helicopter to cross the Sierra Leone River from Lungi Airport to the capital. There had been reports of such old helicopter falling into the river below. But that never bothered my mind. I was more determined to achieve a corporate goal than to consider my security.

The assignment was monumental. I drew a plan that included:

- replacing the IT infrastructure
- installing new servers and desktop PCs for Tellers, Support Staff and Managers.
- converting the database to support the new emerging markets platform being introduced
- training all staff
- building a new secure Data Center
- running all system and user acceptance tests
- cutting over to the new system on a single conversion weekend
- reopening the bank the following Monday

We worked through curfews, slept in the bank when we couldn't leave before lockdown, and operated with a level of intensity that only crisis brings.

Three days after go-live, an audit confirmed data integrity across all accounts. The Country CEO looked at me, exhaled deeply, and said:

"James, you just saved this bank from permanent closure."

They called me a hero.

I didn't feel like one.

I felt tired — and strangely hollow.

I had risked my life for a bank, in a country where I hadn't even ensured my own safety. In hindsight, it was foolish. At the time, it felt like duty.

FIXER AND SAVIOR

Barely three days after returning to Accra, I was sent again — this time to Zimbabwe. A nationwide transformation project had stalled. The IT workstream couldn't deliver a stable infrastructure or a resilient Data Center, and the business simulation tests were failing repeatedly. The project had exceeded budget and there was panic everywhere.

There was no room for error. I marshalled technical assistance from Ghana. In three painful weeks, the expanded team delivered results. The new system went live. I returned to my base station to continue driving for excellence.

I sketched blueprints of backup processes, disaster-recovery plans, audit controls, and re-engineered workflows. We achieved ISO9001 certification for my department — the only such accolade in the bank at the time.

I learned to think like three people at once:

- an engineer (to build)
- an investigator (to question)
- and a pessimist (to foresee what could go wrong)

I used to joke that my job was "imagining disasters professionally." The more successful we were, the less visible the work became. When systems run smoothly, no one asks why.

But let one system fail — and everyone knows your name.

POWER AND ISOLATION

The higher I rose, the fewer people I could talk to honestly.

Sometimes I missed the early days — debugging code with colleagues, restoring historic data, laughing over late-night chicken dinners. Now I monitored systems across six countries, tracing logs and access patterns while trying not to lose touch with the people behind them — the support staff and telecoms specialists who jumped out of bed at midnight when I called, to fix a failing server.

> "When you become the gatekeeper, you stop feeling like a citizen of the city you protect."

THE PARADOX OF JOB SECURITY

Security is built on the illusion of control.

You tell yourself that if every firewall stands, every password holds, every report is perfect — the world is safe. But true job security doesn't live in systems.

It lives in you.

I learned that senior executives were "castle builders" — strategists whose careers were propelled by the technical experts protecting the foundation. I secured systems worth millions, yet I hadn't built any security for myself.

- No investments
- No personal safety net
- No backup plan for my own life

I had backups for data but none for my dreams.

A MOMENT OF TRUTH

One evening, during a group audit debrief, a regional executive credited a consulting firm for implementing "the new system security framework."

It was a framework I developed with my team — every clause, every slide, every control.

I watched the applause roll across the room.

I smiled outwardly, silent inwardly.

Once again, I had built something that belonged to everyone but those who did the work.

That night, alone, I asked myself:

"How did I become so indispensable yet so replaceable?"

The answer came quietly:

Because I had never owned the value I created.

TRANSLATING LESSONS INTO LIFE

I started keeping a different kind of notebook — not for incidents or audits, but for principles:

- **Redundancy** → multiple income streams
- **Disaster Recovery** → emergency savings
- **Access Control** → boundaries
- **Risk Appetite** → knowing how far uncertainty could stretch before peace collapses

What began as a systems-resilience philosophy became a life philosophy.

THE BLUEPRINT FOR MY FUTURE

I saw the truth with sudden clarity:

I had spent years safeguarding institutions that could replace me in a day.

Yet no one was safeguarding me.

Security wasn't about tightening locks.

It was about building **exits you control.**

No one was safeguarding me because everyone at the senior or executive level was busy trying to secure themselves. That's how it is in the corporate world.

That realization would guide everything that followed — my financial discipline, my career decisions, and the blueprint for a life not dependent on corporate applause. Still, I had to keep going – working with pride and dignity.

CHAPTER 5

THE PARADOX OF SUCCESS

I arrived in Lagos knowing two things: first, the assignment was politically sensitive; second, the situation on the ground was far more complex than the polished reports circulating at headquarters. I had been sent to set up a new franchise of the parent bank where none existed. I was the Lead Project Manager with the experience and knowledge of what a live operating bank looked like: secure, efficient, modern and reliable. What I didn't know was that this trip would become one of the defining experiences of my career — the moment when the illusion of corporate success finally cracked.

The first warning sign came the moment I stepped out of Murtala Muhammed Airport and sensed a tension I couldn't quite name — a tension in the air, in the body language of the driver sent to collect me, in the unusual quiet on the way to Victoria Island. Something wasn't right. And it didn't take long before someone pulled me aside and whispered that my presence was not welcomed by everyone involved in the project. In fact, some felt threatened.

I shouldn't have been surprised. Banks don't send in "fixers" unless something is deeply wrong. And when you arrive as the fixer, someone somewhere has already decided that you are the replacement — or the verdict.

Yet I did what I always did: focused on the work. I spent long hours in my hotel room, reviewing my project plan, examining dependencies on external contractors, realigning processes, assessing the security in Victoria Island, and reassuring my family in Accra that I was safe. I didn't eat well. I didn't sleep well. But quietly, the pieces started falling into place. Within a week, I had gotten the project, recruited IT staff who I rapidly sent out to Gambia, Zimbabwe and Ghana for training in the new system they will have to manage upon their return. I coordinated electrical contractors, networks and telecoms contractors. I produced a sub-project plan which dove-tailed into the main project. Executives in London praised that move as "decisive."

Then came the moment that stays with me even now.

On the morning of a high-level review meeting, soon after the bank had been successfully opened to the public, the newly appointed CEO seriously questioned my decision in recruiting the various IT support roles in the bank I built – a similar project I successfully managed in La Cote d'Ivoire a few months earlier. He even requested to see the resumes of the said staff. Beyond their IT skills, I evaluated each of them for "silent" qualities like honesty, reliability, loyalty and integrity. Fifteen years on, those staff are still serving the bank.

I had gone from being the person sent to set up a greenfield bank to a person that needed to be discredited.

I had built success others wanted to own — without me.

This was the moment I first understood what I now call **the corporate paradox:**

**When you perform exceptionally well,
you become both valuable and vulnerable.**

The more you solve, the more you're watched.

The more visible you become, the more exposed you are to people who project their failures onto you.

I brushed past that incident. I provided the resumes and never discussed the matter. I focused on successfully completing the project and return to my base station. But the damage was done. Not to the project. The damage was internal. A shift had begun.

I completed the assignment with the same professionalism I brought to every job. The bank praised my contribution. They said I had "delivered" one of the most difficult greenfield projects in the region.

But on the flight back to Accra, sitting by the window as the plane lifted through the heavy Lagos haze, I realized I felt empty. Not defeated — just empty. I had done everything right. I had delivered. I represented the bank with loyalty, discipline, and courage.

And yet, somewhere in the process of building stability for the institution, I had begun to lose stability within myself.

I thought of the long hours, the missed family moments, the late-night crisis calls, the silent sacrifices no one sees. I thought about how easily one can be excluded from a system they helped build.

Then, for the first time in my career, a quiet question formed in my mind:

"If I can do all this — if I can build banks, stabilize operations, and rescue failing systems — why can't I build something of my own?"

It was a question that stayed with me for years — the beginning of an awakening.

A reminder that competence, by itself, is not a strategy.

And that loyalty, without self-preservation, is a slow form of erosion.

I landed in Accra with one truth echoing in my mind:

Success inside the institution does not always translate into success outside it.

This chapter of my life proved that even when you reach the peak of your competence, if you do not build parallel strength in your personal life, you can climb high yet remain fragile.

And that realization became the seed of everything that followed.

CHAPTER 6

THE SILENT EXIT

Back in Accra, I was completing the building of a world-class Regional Data Center where all servers for the region were housed. It served as a systems hub for all six countries in West Africa as well as a backup Data Center for East Africa.

The air-conditioned chill, the glass partitions, the humming printers — everything was fresh and satisfying. But something inside me had crossed an invisible line. The badge on my chest still opened doors, yet it no longer symbolized belonging. I had stopped believing that the next promotion would fix anything.

There was no announcement, no declaration, no crisis.

My exit began a few weeks later, when I walked into my office and felt... nothing.

That is how every real departure begins — not with a resignation letter, but with the moment you detach emotionally while still showing up physically. The institution still owns your time, but it no longer owns your conviction.

And then the small signs appear.

When "cost-cutting" suddenly removes benefits that used to be standard.

When expansion plans dry up with no explanation.

When silence grows thicker than any official announcement.

Then came the final cue: my boss casually asked me to recommend a senior manager "from anywhere in the world" who could provide leadership like I did. That was the moment I knew I was being replaced. Months earlier, I had quietly refused his instruction to fire my most knowledgeable UNIX specialist with no tangible reason linked to technical incompetence or negligence. This engineer maintained all the servers in the Data Center. Removing him would have been organizational suicide. I protected him because it was the right thing to do.

When you manage mission-critical systems, not only must you master the workflows, but your decision-making must also be professional and fearless. You are accountable for every decision you make.

But in banking, principles often collide with politics.

My stance had been noted. The consequence was to follow.

Still, my own exit plans were already in motion.

Resignation isn't a letter; it's a mindset.

**And it begins the day you stop believing
the next title will save you.**

THE DECISION BEHIND CLOSED DOORS

I made no sudden moves. No one does — not in corporate life.

You plan your exit the same way you build a risk-mitigation strategy: quietly, thoroughly, and with redundancies. By the time you walk out of the door, the emotional exit has long been completed.

I had already begun preparing my unit managers. We reviewed processes, updated documentation, strengthened operational frameworks — not for the auditors this time, but for my own peace. Then I recommended a former colleague I had worked with and known as competent. They hired him quickly. He was to replace me.

At night, during my quiet moments, I built a different kind of checklist — one for my personal transition:

- Kids' schooling
- Housing stability
- Review savings horizon
- Build a six-month reserve
- Study small-business structures

I wasn't creating an escape plan.

I was designing an exit.

THE INVISIBLE BRIDGE

Money was never the enemy.

Dependence was.

Walking away without a safety net turns liberation into panic. So I treated financial independence like a sub-project. Each act of planning was a small step away from fear.

I read obsessively — books on entrepreneurship, dividend port-folios, early retirement psychology. I learned that wealth isn't the number on your payslip.

Wealth is the distance between your needs and your peace.

Slowly, a bridge began taking shape — one spreadsheet cell at a time. Each cell felt like reclaiming a part of myself I had ignored for far too long.

THE MENTORSHIP SEASON

As my exit took form, something unexpected happened:

I began to see my sixty-plus staff not as functional components of an operating system, but as people.

Maybe it was because I knew the system could grind enthusiasm into compliance. Maybe it was because I wished someone had protected me when I was younger. Either way, I shifted from managing them to *growing* them.

I shared stories HR would never tell — about moral courage,

about saying no without apology, about maintaining your humanity inside a corporate machine.

At one monthly meeting, I quoted a line I had once read:

"Every job is a self-portrait of the person who did it.
Autograph your work with excellence."

Years later, when I visited the team in Accra, they proudly showed me that statement — enlarged, framed, and mounted on the wall of their Service Delivery office.

In that moment, I realized something profound:

My legacy was no longer tied to the position I held.
It was tied to the people I had grown.
The Farewell They Never Saw Coming

When the day finally came, I delivered my handover notes with the same calm precision I used for audit sign-offs. No anger. No drama. Just clarity and gratitude.

The news travelled quickly.

"Are you serious?" one executive asked.

"You're leaving now — when everything is opening up for you?"

I smiled.

"That's exactly why."

I packed the few personal items from my drawer — notebooks, loose pens, a globe-shaped stress ball. I took the stairs down for the last time. At the exit, security nodded. I nodded back.

There was no confetti.

No farewell speeches.

Just silence — the kind that feels like truth.

FREEDOM AND DISORIENTATION

Freedom is not a moment. It is a series of quiet mornings.

The first week felt strange. I still woke up early, checked my email out of habit, and felt a small ache where urgency used to live. By the second week, the silence softened. I walked without headphones. I read during breakfast. I heard my own thoughts again.

But I still measured time in deliverables. It takes months to unlearn that.

Sometimes I missed the structure — not the meetings, but the momentum. Then I understood something:

**Discipline is not owned by institutions.
It is a skill you take with you.**

The world remained the same, but I was not.

REFLECTION — REDEFINING THE EXIT

Looking back, leaving was not rejection. It was alignment.

I didn't leave the bank.

I outgrew the version of myself that needed it.

Real exits are not dramatic. They are deliberate. You don't burn bridges; you quietly build new ones. You leave the noise behind with dignity, carrying only the lessons that serve your next chapter.

I didn't leave because the bank was broken.

I left because — for the first time — **I was whole.**

And that realization planted the seed for something greater: a desire to build systems not for corporations, but for people like me — professionals seeking balance, agency, and a blueprint for purposeful independence.

CHAPTER 7

THE BLUEPRINT OF FREEDOM

The first morning after I left the bank felt unreal.

The sun streamed through the blinds just as it had every other day, but something fundamental had shifted. There was no calendar shaping my morning, no dawn meeting hovering over my thoughts, no silence broken by the vibration of an early call. I stood by the window with a cup of coffee, unsure how to live in a world that did not demand urgency from me.

For the first time in years, I had nothing to rush toward.

And strangely, that frightened me.

My body still behaved as though deadlines were waiting on the other side of the door. I checked my phone reflexively, forgetting that no escalations were coming. But beneath that unease was something gentler — a quiet invitation to rebuild my relationship with time.

Freedom doesn't arrive with fireworks.

It whispers.

And to hear it, you must slow down.

THE FIRST MORNING
WITHOUT A CALENDAR

For weeks, I continued waking up before sunrise out of habit. Years of corporate conditioning had trained my mind to anticipate demand. Waking to a day without structure felt like attending a meeting with no agenda — disorienting at first, but soon unexpectedly liberating.

The silence grew into spaciousness.

I filled it with thought, then with writing — small reflections, brief notes, even diagrams. My children's morning routines became no longer a logistical challenge but a joy. For the first time in my working life, I could take them to school and pick them up. That alone felt like a luxury no salary had ever granted me.

The absence of a schedule became room to design a new kind of life.

The same discipline I had once applied to the bank's systems, I now turned inward.

For the first time, **I was the project.**

FROM STRUCTURE TO STRATEGY

Leaving the institution revealed something I had never fully recognized: my value was not in the bank's hierarchy — it was in my ability to manage complexity.

That was the invisible capital I carried out of the building.

So, I used it. I began designing my days the way I once designed multi-country service operations — with balance, clarity, and purpose. I divided my time into portfolios:

- Strategic (future-building decisions)
- Creative (writing, thinking, exploring ideas)
- Personal (family, health, reflection)

I even built dashboards. Not for uptime or performance indicators, but for myself — what I was reading, how much I was writing, how present I was with my family.

In the bank, I had built systems that kept institutions alive.

In freedom, I started building systems that kept *me* alive.

THE INTELLECTUAL PIVOT

Freedom awakened a hunger in me — not for rest, but for learning.

For years, my reading diet had been functional: regulatory updates, risk reports, project methodologies. Now, I read out of curiosity. Psychology, economics, urban farming, spirituality, design thinking — subjects that reconnected me to wonder.

I rediscovered questions that didn't fit into dashboards or KPIs.

My curiosity returned with surprising force.

Ideas for ventures, models, and programs began forming spontaneously.

My analytical mind hadn't retired; it had simply been reassigned.

I had shifted from **compliance to curiosity**, and it changed everything.

DESIGNING THE BLUEPRINT

One quiet afternoon, I sat at my desk — the very space that had once carried performance reviews and audit reports — and began to draw. Not pictures, but architecture.

A framework.

A personal operating system.

My **Blueprint of Freedom**.

It began with five circles:

1. Financial Independence
Smart, simple investments.
Small ventures.
Franchising ideas.
Income streams that prioritized *control* over *size*.

2. Intellectual Growth
Read.
Think.
Research.
Write.
Growth wasn't tethered to profit.

3. Community Impact
Mentorship.
Listening.
Volunteering.
Knowledge-sharing in ways the corporate world had no space for.

4. Health and Presence
A return to balance — body, mind, nature, faith, empathy, patience.

5. Creative Expression
Work that spoke to purpose instead of policy.
Under each circle, I wrote small, practical actions — nothing ambitious, just daily proof of direction. In the bank, I learned to mitigate risk.
In freedom, I learned to *tackle* it.

THE FINANCIAL FRAMEWORK

Outside banking, money revealed its real meaning: **control, not consumption**.

I simplified my life.

Budgeted tightly.

Reduced waste.

Focused spending on intention.

Every dollar not wasted became a dollar earned for autonomy.

My revenue streams grew slowly but with purpose — consulting here, a workshop there, a small venture taking shape.

Freedom without structure is chaos.

Structure without freedom is a cage.

The brilliance lies in the balance.

COMMUNITY AND CONNECTION

It's a myth that independence means isolation.

The opposite happened.

I began reconnecting with people I had lost to corporate schedules — former colleagues, founders, academics, neighbors, and sometimes strangers who became friends. Conversations were unfiltered. No titles. No performance agendas.

Some became clients.

Others mentors.

A few became mirrors.

Networks built on authenticity outlast those built on ambition.

THE ETHICAL CORE

Freedom tests integrity in a new way.

Inside institutions, ethics is compliance.

Outside institutions, ethics is conviction.

There were no auditors now, no governance meetings or HR

policies. Every decision was self-governed. I learned to choose projects not by profit, but by alignment.

Mentorship continued too — but with a different gravity.

I wasn't representing a bank anymore.

I was representing lessons hard-earned.

It mattered more.

FREEDOM AS RESPONSIBILITY

It took months to understand that freedom wasn't rest — it was stewardship.

A year after leaving the bank, I opened my first modern grocery store. It launched beautifully. And then it failed — after ten months.

There was no team to blame, no process to critique, no policy loophole to cite.

The lesson was simple and sharp:

Outside the institution, you are the system.

Success or failure traces back to you and you alone.

But that accountability was liberating.

Because ownership, even of mistakes, is the purest form of control.

"You don't escape the system; you evolve into a better one."

Seven years later, I attempted the grocery store initiative again but this time as franchise business model. It is still running and expanding.

REFLECTION — THE ARCHITECTURE OF CHOICE

Looking back, I didn't abandon structure — I redefined it.

The corporate world taught me to build stability.

Freedom taught me to build *possibility*.

And the difference is not in the systems we construct,

but in who owns them.

This chapter marked a gentle turning point — the moment leadership became less about holding institutions together and more about understanding the cost of staying too long in places we have outgrown.

What I carried forward was not the weight of responsibility,

but the clarity that purpose must evolve — and that freedom is something we build long before we walk away.

And now that I had designed my freedom, a new question emerged:

What will I do with it — even now?

CHAPTER 8

THE CURRENCY OF IMPACT

Legacy is a quiet thing.

You never really know what you leave behind until long after you've stepped away — sometimes years later, sometimes in places you never expect.

I spent most of my corporate years believing impact meant achievements, metrics, projects completed, systems stabilized, crises resolved. I thought legacy lived in dashboards and performance reviews. But as life would prove, none of those things endure. Not really. Not in the ways that matter.

The true currency of impact is people.

You invest in them without knowing whether the return will come in months, years, or decades — or whether it will come at all. And often, it isn't until you've moved on, sometimes far beyond the walls where the work was done, that the evidence quietly reveals itself.

THE ECHOES YOU DON'T EXPECT

Months after I stepped away from the bank, I traveled through Accra and decided — almost on a whim — to stop by the old office. I didn't go inside. I simply stood across the street and watched the building. Life continued as though I had never been a part of it. People rushed in and out. Security guards waved cars forward. The world moved.

Nothing in that moment suggested my presence had ever mattered.

But legacy doesn't announce itself through buildings.

It surfaces through people.

A few days later, I received a message from a former team member — one of the quiet, diligent analysts who rarely spoke in meetings but always delivered. She was now leading the very unit she once supported. She wrote:

> **"Sir, everything you taught us is still here.**
> **Your principles run this department."**

No award in my entire career carried more meaning than that single sentence.

THE LONG ROOTS OF LEADERSHIP

I've come to understand that impact often grows underground. You don't see the roots forming. You don't witness the slow strengthening of the people you've mentored, encouraged, challenged, sometimes corrected, and sometimes carried.

The investment happens in moments so ordinary you barely remember them:

- explaining a system flaw while someone quietly takes notes
- guiding a junior colleague through a difficult decision
- defending someone who cannot defend themselves
- restoring confidence to a team after a failure

- choosing ethics over shortcuts
- keeping someone's dignity intact

These moments feel small.

But they are not.

They are seeds.

Some fall on hard soil and never take hold.

But others — the ones that land in ready hearts — grow into forests.

THE WEIGHT OF RESPONSIBILITY

Leadership without maturity is noise.

Leadership without compassion is damage.

Leadership without humility is a wound that never heals.

The older I became, the more I recognized that real leadership is not what you do when everyone is watching. It is what you build when no one pays attention — when you choose integrity in a room full of shortcuts, when you protect someone's future despite the political cost, when you decide that work must serve humanity before it serves the institution.

I didn't always get it right.

No leader does.

But I tried — genuinely — to ensure that the people who worked under my guidance left stronger than when they arrived. And as the years passed, that intention mattered more than any system I built or any crisis I solved.

WHAT REMAINS AFTER YOU LEAVE

The titles fade.

The emails stop.

The corporate memory resets.

The institution continues.

You are replaced — sometimes quickly, sometimes silently.

But what remains are the people you lifted.

People who gained courage because you defended them at the right time.

People who discovered their potential because you expected more of them.

People who learned discipline, dignity, and resilience not from training manuals, but from watching how you handled pressure, conflict, and uncertainty.

Some of those individuals still carry the lessons.

Some pass them on to others.

And those others will pass them on again.

That is impact — exponential, invisible, enduring.

LEGACY, REFRAMED

In my early career, I believed legacy was what I accomplished.

In my mid-career, I believed legacy was what I built.

But now I understand:

Legacy is who you strengthen.
Legacy is who you free.
Legacy is who becomes better because you were there.

The institutions I served will outlive me.

But so will the people I helped shape — and that is enough.

This chapter taught me the most important lesson of all:

Your true value is not determined by the corporation you work for.

It is determined by the lives you influence along the way.

And if you lead well — with courage, honesty, clarity, and kindness —

you leave behind echoes that continue long after your badge stops opening doors.

CHAPTER 9

LESSONS FROM
THE BROKEN VAULT

The training room was quiet now. The presentation slides had faded from the screen, the charts were closed, and the staff clustered in small circles, talking softly among themselves. Their earlier energy had settled into the reflective hush that follows deep learning.

As I packed my notes, a young woman — no more than twenty-five, bright, curious, one of those analysts whose eyes reveal both ambition and hunger — approached me.

"Sir," she asked gently, "if you could go back and start again, what would you do differently?"

Her question hung in the air longer than she expected. Not because I lacked an answer, but because it touched the very part of my life I had spent years understanding — the vault I once believed held the secret to success.

I smiled, not out of certainty, but recognition.

"I would build my future as carefully as I reconcile suspense accounts," I told her. "But I would never again confuse a balanced account with progress."

That conversation became the seed of this chapter — a quiet debrief after a long journey.

Below are the lessons I wish someone had shared with me when I was her age, standing at the edge of possibility, unaware of the vault I was walking into.

LESSON 1 — DON'T CONFUSE EMPLOYMENT WITH OWNERSHIP

When you work in banking, you're surrounded by vast sums of money — wealth greater than most will ever witness. It becomes easy to mistake proximity for participation. You authorize million-dollar transactions, design systems that move markets, approve credit lines that could transform a company's future.

For a while, it feels like those numbers belong to you.

But they don't.

You are an instrument, not a beneficiary.

The institution owns the flow; you maintain the pipes.

The smartest professionals I met weren't the ones chasing promotions. They were the ones quietly building personal ownership alongside their careers — investing in learning, in land, in small ventures that would one day outlive their job titles.

If I could speak to every young banker today, I would say this:

> **Respect your job. Be the absolute best at your job, but build your own vault.**

Do not spend your life securing the institution's assets while neglecting your own.

LESSON 2 — LEARN THE LANGUAGE OF MONEY EARLY

I mastered the mechanics of banking long before I understood the philosophy of money. I wrote code to generate accurate account statement without appreciating what those line entries mean in reality. The algorithm was perfect. The author was financially ignorant.

I could recite compliance rules, KPIs, and audit frameworks — yet I didn't know how real wealth grows. I learned, far too late, that money increases not through effort alone, but through time, patience, and compounding.

Money isn't just earned.

It's managed.

It's translated from energy into options.

The sooner you learn the language of money, the more freedom you will buy later. Study it like learning a second language — because if you don't, someone else will always be fluent enough to make decisions for you.

LESSON 3 — DELIVER

Corporate systems are designed to extract your best gifts — your intelligence, discipline, creativity — for goals that belong to someone else.

There is no shame in this; it is how institutions function.

The tragedy is when you forget to repurpose those same abilities for your own life.

The systems thinking that made me effective as a banking and technology leader later became the backbone of my consulting work. The communication skills I honed in executive meetings became the voice of my mentorship programs. The crisis-management mindset I developed during server failures and high-pressure projects became the calm I carried into seasons of transition.

A skill loses half its power when it serves only one employer.

So treat your career as a laboratory — not a cage.

LESSON 4 – NETWORKS ARE THE REAL CAPITAL

At every stage of my life, relationships opened doors that degrees could not.

I once believed that hard work and intelligence would guarantee advancement. But systems are human, and in human systems, trust moves faster than talent.

Your relationships — mentors, colleagues, peers, even competitors — form a network that will either elevate or limit your future.

Cultivate it with sincerity.

Offer help without hidden agendas.

Be remembered for integrity, not opportunism.

In today's world, where information and digital currencies move in seconds, one truth remains: **capital flows to trust faster than to talent.**

And long after your title fades, your character will continue to speak for you.

LESSON 5 – GUARD YOUR INTEGRITY AS A CURRENCY

Systems collapse.

Institutions fall.

Markets shift without warning.

The only currency that endures every crisis is your reputation.

During my years in banking, shortcuts often appeared tempting — small, seemingly harmless compromises. But integrity rarely breaks in large cracks; it erodes quietly, decision by decision.

Your credibility is the most valuable account you will ever manage.

Once overdrawn, it is almost impossible to restore.

When your name stands for something, opportunities find you — even long after you've left the vault.

LESSON 6 — BALANCE SPEED WITH SUBSTANCE

This lesson is for the new generation — the brilliant Gen-Z minds sprinting into corporate life with caffeine, ambition, and speed.

Speed feels like progress.

But progress is not always direction.

I sprinted too — chasing titles, bonuses, deliverables, travel approvals. I gained motion, yes, but I lost meaning. Mastery requires stillness. Growth requires roots.

Learn deeply.

Invest wisely.

Build slowly.

Patience isn't delay, it's design.

Start a well-researched business that grows in the background. Build investment portfolios that work while you sleep. Create systems that last beyond performance cycles.

You can accelerate your rise,

but you cannot shortcut your becoming.

Build your investment portfolio or operate your side business within the code of conduct of your institution. No insider-dealing, no "flying below the radar". You will be exposed.   And remember, you may need the institution itself as a client when you're all set.

LESSON 7 – REDEFINE WEALTH BEFORE IT REDEFINES YOU

I once built systems worth millions and expanded a bank whose net worth was larger than some countries' budgets — yet I remained poor in the one currency that matters most: peace.

True wealth is freedom.

The freedom to choose how you spend your time.

The freedom to align your work with your principles.

The freedom to say "no" without fear.

I used to think wealth was a destination — somewhere I would eventually arrive.

Now I know:

Wealth is presence.

Being here.

Being whole.

Being unafraid to walk away.

Before you chase success, define wealth for yourself. If you don't, the world will define it for you — and charge you interest for the privilege.

REFLECTION — THE BROKEN VAULT

In the end, my journey feels like a vault — once sealed, now open.

It held not gold, but lessons. Lessons about systems, people, purpose, and, most unexpectedly, myself.

The vault never truly broke.

It evolved.

Its doors opened the moment I realized that security is not the same as fulfillment. That a stable career is not the same as a meaningful life. That wealth without peace is just another form of poverty.

Sometimes the vault must break

for you to see what was truly stored inside.

And what I found were the most valuable things I ever built:

Trust.
Courage.
Wisdom.

And the quiet conviction that even when the numbers fade, the principles remain.

THE QUIET BANK

The afternoon light slanted across the marble floor of the head-office branch lobby, soft and familiar. The hum of the lone printer, the faint scent of paper and toner, the quiet chatter between tellers — all sounds I had once known by heart.

I hadn't planned to visit that day. A former colleague from Nigeria — now the CEO — had asked me to stop by, to share a few words with the team. Stepping through the revolving glass doors as a guest rather than staff felt strange at first. The guard at the entrance smiled politely, not recognizing me. I smiled back. It felt right that he didn't.

I walked slowly through the banking hall, past a few new offices, and climbed the straight stairs to the mezzanine floor where I had once presented strategies and conducted basic IT-skills training. The office looked the same — blue tones, polished metal fixtures — yet everything felt lighter, as if my years of striving had finally released their weight.

The systems had moved on, but pieces of me still lived quietly in the routines of the people I had trained.

THE CORRIDOR REVISITED

When I reached the open space near the CEO's office, a few young faces looked up, curious. Some of the long-serving staff recognized me instantly and jumped in excitement. I had always been celebrated not for my rank, but for how I related with them.

After a brief time with the CEO — during which he recalled how the one branch I had set up in Nigeria had grown into 28 branches — I took a last look around: the staff, the screens, the whiteboards, the posters.

Everything had changed, yet nothing had.

And the realization filled me with peace.

THE INVISIBLE BANK

I realized I had never really stopped banking.

I had only changed what I deposited.

Now, I invest in people — in trust, knowledge, and possibility. My new "bank" was invisible, its branches scattered far wider than any institution I had ever worked for.

One "branch" was a small mentorship circle of young professionals across the region, sharing fears about their careers and futures. Another — perhaps the quietest — was my writing: reflections that helped others see meaning again in their daily work.

I still make deposits — only now they are slow, intentional, human.

And their impact reaches further than any system upgrade ever did.

The more I recognized this, the wealthier I felt — a wealth no corporate title had ever given me.

THE SOUND OF LEGACY

Some legacies don't echo loudly.

They hum — gently, consistently — like a well-tuned engine running in the background.

Every now and then, a message finds its way to me:

"Sir, we used your model for this year's audit — it worked beautifully."

"That talk you gave helped me apply for a role I was afraid of."

"Thank you for believing in me when the system didn't."

These are my dividends — quiet returns on long-ago investments in people.

No headlines, no ceremonies. Just reminders that the systems I once built were always meant to serve the human spirit within them.

Living in the U.S. now, the same telecommunications technology that once held me captive in service of the bank now connects me to mentees everywhere. Recently, one sent me pictures of his new line of work — something we had never discussed. As we exchanged messages, I told him:

"Fantastic. I am impressed. Keep up the good work. Be professional in everything you do. It is your turn to shine.

ESSAY ONE – ON AMBITION AND QUIET LOSS

Ambition is rarely the enemy. It is often the companion that carries us forward when confidence is fragile and opportunity uncertain. Yet ambition, when left unchecked, can quietly hollow out the very life it was meant to build.

In my corporate years, ambition taught me discipline, resilience, and speed. It also taught me how easily rest becomes guilt, how identity becomes conditional, and how worth slowly attaches itself to performance alone. The danger was not the work itself, but the silence that followed each achievement — the moment when the next goal appeared before the previous one could even be felt.

This essay is not a rejection of ambition, but an invitation to interrogate it. To ask whether the ladder we climb is leaning against a wall we would still choose if no one were watching.

ESSAY TWO – MENTORSHIP IS NOT MANAGEMENT

The most influential figures in my career were rarely my managers. They were mentors — often unofficial, sometimes invisible, always human.

Management ensures delivery. Mentorship ensures growth.

In complex institutions, mentorship is often undervalued because it does not appear on performance dashboards. Yet it is mentorship that transfers wisdom, not just process; discernment, not just compliance. I learned most when someone took the time to explain *why* a decision mattered — not merely *what* needed to be done.

For young professionals, seeking mentors is not weakness. It is strategy. And for leaders, offering mentorship is not generosity — it is responsibility.

ESSAY THREE – REDEFINING WEALTH BEFORE IT IS TOO LATE

If I could speak to my younger self, I would not warn him about failure. I would warn him about postponement.

Postponement of rest.

Postponement of joy.

Postponement of self.

Wealth, as I understand it now, is not the accumulation of assets alone, but the preservation of agency — the ability to choose, to pause, to walk away when necessary. True wealth allows space for dignity.

This essay is a reminder that no salary compensates for a life lived entirely in anticipation of a future that never quite arrives.

LESSONS FOR THE MODERN PROFESSIONAL

1. Entering Corporate Life: Foundations for Young Professionals

The first years of your career are where your habits, reputation, and identity take shape. It is not enough to understand your academic field; you must expand your knowledge of the *industry ecosystem* you are entering. Learn how your company fits into the wider market, how decisions flow, and how value is created.

Key principles:

- Understand the corporate objective. Know what the business values, tracks, and rewards.
- Become known for dependability. Let colleagues experience you as someone who delivers results consistently.
- Build humility-based relationships. Be approachable, respectful, and human — not subservient.
- Manage your time with discipline. Treat urgency as a professional language.

A reputation formed early can carry — or haunt — you for years.

2. Developing Technical Identity: From Analyst to Problem-Solver

Early in my own banking journey, I discovered that competence is not just what you already know — it is how quickly you adapt.

I had been a coder in another bank, but in this new environment, strict access controls meant I could no longer "fix" issues through code. Parameter files, access rules, and tightly controlled change processes left me feeling restricted.

So I turned to another strength: problem analysis.

When recurring issues frustrated customers monthly and no one could resolve them, I volunteered to investigate. I analysed data, parameter files, and workflow logic until I discovered a sustainable fix — all within the boundaries of what analysts were permitted to touch.

Lesson:

Every organization has unsolved problems that everyone avoids.

Solve one — and you immediately earn respect, visibility, and trust.

This is how you establish yourself not merely as staff, but as *a contributor who matters.*

3. Rising Into Middle Management: Becoming a People Leader

Promotion introduces its own complexity. Suddenly, technical skill is no longer enough — you are now responsible for people, execution, morale, and cohesion.

Guidance for this stage:

- Study your job description but don't be limited by it.

Know the full scope of your function.

- Acquire soft skills intentionally: communication, managing change, conflict resolution, and people development.
- Align with corporate goals. Seek clarity from your manager regularly.
- Lead with fairness and professionalism. Your influence grows not by authority alone, but by credibility.

Management is not about control — it is about enabling others to succeed.

4. Regional Exposure and International Assignments: Operating Across Borders

When I began supporting service management and project rollouts in other countries, I realized how much leadership depends on understanding context.

The rules here are simple but powerful:

- Be loyal to the organization, not factions. Avoid internal politics.
- Learn local culture, social norms, and communication styles. Respect builds bridges.
- Use interpersonal skills to achieve outcomes. You cannot dictate across borders; you must influence.
- Appraise performance honestly and professionally. Your integrity becomes your passport.

To thrive internationally, you must learn to lead without relying on positional power.

CLOSING REFLECTION

Across all levels — analyst, manager, international lead — the same truth remains:

Your career grows when you grow.

Skills alone are not enough; identity, purpose, and discipline must grow with them.

ACKNOWLEDGEMENTS

This book is the product of journeys across countries, institutions, and seasons of my life. I am deeply grateful to the people who walked with me, challenged me, encouraged me, and helped me find clarity long before I found the words to tell this story.

To colleagues and friends in **Zimbabwe, Kenya, Zambia, Ghana, Nigeria, London, The Gambia, Cameroon, and beyond** — thank you for shaping my growth and leaving an imprint of resilience and excellence on my life.

To the leaders who believed in my abilities, often before I believed in them myself — thank you for the opportunities and lessons.

To my family, thank you for your patience, love, and grounding presence.

And to you, the reader — thank you for stepping into this story.

These lessons are not theories.

They are lived experience — paid for in time, energy, mistakes, and ultimately, wisdom.

ABOUT THE AUTHOR

James Roberts holds a Bachelor's degree in Computer Science with Economics, a Master's degree in Project Management, and a second Master's degree in Health Informatics. His work bridges technology, leadership, and human-centered systems across global institutions.

www.ingramcontent.com/pod-product-compliance
Lightning Source LLC
Chambersburg PA
CBHW020313150626
46552CB00022B/2868